3 00
Br

Mon Docteur le Vin

(My Doctor, Wine)

Mon Docteur le Vin

(My Doctor, Wine)

WATERCOLORS BY

Raoul Dufy

TEXT BY GASTON DERYS

INTRODUCTION BY PAUL LUKACS

TRANSLATED BY BENJAMIN IVRY

DISTRIBUTED BY
YALE UNIVERSITY PRESS
NEW HAVEN AND LONDON
FOR THE HENRY McBRIDE CHARITABLE TRUST

Raoul Dufy's illustrations © 2003 Artists Rights Society (ARS), New York / ADAGP, Paris.

Printed in China by C & C Offset Printing Co., Ltd.

Library of Congress Cataloging-in-Publication Data
Derys, Gaston, 1875–
[Mon Docteur le vin. English]
My doctor, wine / text by Gaston Derys; watercolors by Raoul Dufy;
introduction by Paul Lukacs; translated by Benjamin Ivry.
    p.   cm.
French text originally published in 1936.
ISBN 0-300-10133-3 (cloth: alk. paper)
1. Wine—Therapeutic use. 2. Wine and wine making. I. Title.
RM256.D4413 2003
615.8'54—dc21   2003006939

A catalogue record for this book is available from the British Library.

The paper in this book meets the guidelines for permanence and durability of the Committee on Production Guidelines for Book Longevity of the Council on Library Resources.

10 9 8 7 6 5 4 3 2 1

My Doctor, Wine? . . .

You bet,
since science validates
these age-old precepts
more and more each day.

In Tribute to Wine

Of all the supplies sent to our army during the war, wine was surely the most highly anticipated and appreciated by soldiers.

In order to get some "plonk," our "dogfaces" would risk danger, face down shells, and scoff at the military police. To them, supplies of wine were almost as vital as supplies of ammunition.

For our fighting forces, wine was a beneficent stimulant of morale as well as of physical strength. Thus it contributed significantly—in its own way—to the victory.

July 27, 1935
Marshal Pétain

CONTENTS

Introduction

Paul Lukacs

Mon Docteur le Vin, first published in Paris in 1936, was the brainchild of Étienne Nicolas, the innovative director of the chain of wine shops that carries his family name to this day. In essence an advertisement, the book was designed to promote a specific image of French wine, and hence to help sell wines made in that image. Nicolas wanted to present wine as something healthy and natural, and at the same time cultured and refined—which is exactly what the combination of Gaston Derys's prose and Raoul Dufy's art does. Derys, quoting from scientific authorities, offers ostensibly factual evidence of wine's nourishing properties, while Dufy provides glimpses of elegant haute-bourgeoisie leisure. His paintings do not depict people drinking wine. In fact, only two contain images of wine at all. Instead, the illustrations are of wine's effects: civilized health and happiness hand in hand. This would be but a pretty piece of propaganda were it not for the fact that the book plays a small part in a much larger story, that of the changing face of wine in French and indeed all Western culture. More than most of his colleagues in the wine trade at the time, Étienne Nicolas foresaw that the new guarantees of authenticity being legislated in France would lead to new standards of wine quality and, equally important, new habits of appreciation. And he wanted his stores to profit from the change. *Mon Docteur le Vin* did not advertise the Nicolas shops or even the wines sold there. Instead, it simply promoted wine. But it did so in a way designed to bring customers to his door.

The first Nicolas shop opened in 1822. By 1900 the company had grown to include 42 stores in and around Paris. Étienne Nicolas assumed control of the firm after the First World War, and he oversaw a period of tremendous expansion all throughout France—180 stores in 1922; 233 by 1932; 304 in 1936.[1] (There are some 400 today, along with 25 in England and a few others in Belgium, Germany, and Poland.) This growth coincided with a surge in French wine consumption; in the decades from 1920 to 1940 more wine was drunk than ever before in the country's history—a rate approaching the astounding figure of 250 liters per adult each year.[2] Though Nicolas certainly profited from the fact that people were drinking so much wine, the growth of his business reflected something else. The Nicolas chain featured fine wine as opposed to *vin ordinaire,* wine from specific appellations as opposed to generic *vin de pays.* These stores had been among the first to sell wine by the bottle rather than from tank or barrel, as well as the first to offer customers a range of wines from all the important grape growing regions in France. Since a bottle of Bordeaux or Burgundy of the sort available at a Nicolas shop invariably cost more than a jug of generic red sold in a café down the street, Étienne Nicolas needed to convince consumers that the difference in quality justified the higher price. He realized early on that advertising was the way to do it.

The most famous single item of Nicolas advertising was the figure of Nectar, the wide-eyed, mustachioed delivery man, carrying sixteen wine bottles in each hand, who soon became as much a part of French cultural iconography as the round Michelin tire man or the laughing cheese cow. First created in 1921 by the artist Jules Dransy, Nectar served Étienne Nicolas well. The widely recognizable image reminded people that his stores featured bottled, not bulk wines, which they happily delivered to customers' homes. Pictures of Nectar adorned the walls in all the Nicolas shops. Statuettes sat on the counters. More significant, Nectar always was portrayed prominently in the Nicolas catalogues, booklets listing the various wines for sale that customers could use to place orders. These were the result of another of Étienne Nicolas's inspired ideas, as they brought him new customers via a new invention, the home telephone.

The first Nicolas catalogue was issued under Étienne Nicolas's direction in 1925. It proved so successful that he soon supplemented it with a luxury edition, listing only premium wines and offered only to his best clients. In order to distinguish this new volume from his regular catalogue, he decided to commission a different artist to illustrate it each year. (He also began hiring different illustrators to depict Nectar for the regular edition.) Over the years, some of France's most renowned painters and designers worked for him, including A. M. Cassandre and Charles Loupot, and the luxury catalogues became highly sought-after collectibles. At the same time, Nicolas commissioned a series of illustrated gift books on wine-related subjects. Paul Iribe and Charles Martin were among the artists, and a different book appeared just about every year for a decade. *Mon Docteur le Vin* was the last to be published, as the threat of war brought all of Étienne Nicolas's creative advertising to a halt soon afterward.

It is unclear whether Nicolas knew Raoul Dufy personally before contracting for the nineteen watercolors in *Mon Docteur le Vin,* but he certainly knew Dufy's work. By the mid-1930s, that work had achieved considerable renown with the general public, as its luminous colors helped popularize modern art among just the sort of respectable (rather than radical) people whom Nicolas wanted to attract to his stores. As Jean Cocteau reputedly said, Dufy's paintings were offered to the world "like a bouquet."[3] Who better, then, to illustrate a book that often would be given as a gift? Nicolas certainly knew Gaston Derys, one of France's leading gastronomic writers. Derys lived in Paris, where for a time he worked as the associate director of the Galleria museum of fashion and design, and he and Nicolas surely met at various dinners and wine-related events. The author of a number of books on French food and wine, including *L'Art d'Être Gourmand,* he was an obvious choice for *Mon Docteur le Vin.*

The contention that wine can be good for one's health was widely supported by French medical opinion when Derys did his research for the book. Claims that may strike readers as excessive today (wine as a preventive for appendicitis, to name one) would not have seemed so to a contemporary audience. The French

National Academy of Medicine officially distinguished wine from other forms of alcohol. Many doctors maintained that drinking distilled spirits caused alcoholism, with some going so far as to claim that regular wine consumption was the best antidote. An organization of physicians called Medical Friends of the Wines of France actively promoted wine's medicinal properties, and Derys clearly read its literature.[4] (He cites many of its members, including its founder, Doctor Adolphe Portmann, an ear-nose-and-throat specialist from the Gironde.) In short, there was little new or even unexpected in his text.

What was new, or at least surprising, was the marriage of that text with Dufy's art. Most arguments in favor of increased wine consumption in France during the 1930s, whether medical or political, were directed at lower- and middle-class people, primarily men, living in rural areas. But these are hardly the sort of people Dufy depicts in his paintings. Nor are they the sort of clientele to whom Étienne Nicolas catered in his stores. Derys and Dufy may have worked independently and at cross purposes, but it seems more likely that they were inspired or perhaps even instructed by Nicolas to deliver a specific message—not just that wine is good for health, but that wine is good for certain people's health, specifically those people, women as well as men, infected by what Derys calls the snobbery that leads to "intoxication with cocktails and other poisons." After all, those are the people, urban and urbane, haute-bourgeois to the hilt, that Dufy depicts in his paintings, and that Nicolas courted in his shops.

The high rate of wine drinking in the interwar period obscures what was in other respects an identity crisis for French wine. Consumption of all forms of alcohol rose during what the historian Eugen Weber aptly dubs "the hollow years," in large measure as a form of escape.[5] People drank copious amounts of beer and cider in the north, home-distilled liquors in the south, heady aperitifs in cafés everywhere, and, especially in Paris and other cities, imported spirits. Influenced in no small measure by scenes in movies, cocktails became all the rage with the

Parisian smart set. Meanwhile, French vintners faced calamity after calamity. Over-production was the biggest one, as the market became flooded with cheap bulk wine, much of it from Algeria, and prices plummeted. Even though people were drinking more wine, growers in historic appellations lost money. For fine wine producers, the big problem was the loss of customers. Vintners in Bordeaux, Burgundy, or Champagne, the leading exports, saw market after market for their wines disappear. The economies of Germany, Austria, and Hungary were in shambles, devastated by war. Revolution and National Prohibition had eliminated previously profitable markets in Russia and the United States. Even England, long the most reliable purchaser of fine French wine, was buying less. Adding to these difficulties was the increasingly muddled image of French wine—exclusive and elite at the high end, otherwise coarse and crude, a peasant drink. Regular reports of fraud circulated in the press throughout the 1920s, as bottles with prestigious labels turned out to contain cheap, inferior plonk. Then came economic depression, drying up demand even more. The crisis became so acute that vineyard after vineyard was put up for sale, at record low prices. The government had to respond—first, to stem the flow of unwanted bulk wine, and then even more important, to protect the heritage of the country's great wines.

It did, albeit slowly. In a series of decrees issued between 1931 and 1936, the supply of *vin ordinaire* gradually was brought in line with demand. New planting was banned, some vineyards destroyed, unsold wine sent to distilleries, and prolific hybrid grape varieties outlawed. Production fell by more than 10 percent. At the same time, long-standing questions of integrity began to be addressed. In 1935 the Institut National des Appellations d'Origine (INAO) was formed to administer, regulate and protect all fine wine—that is, all wine coming from controlled appellations. This was precisely the sort of wine Étienne Nicolas sold in his shops, precisely the sort of wine that Derys and Dufy's book contended was so good for one's health.

The establishment of the INAO was a long time coming. France's reputation as the preeminent European wine-producing country had been severely damaged—first, by a series of viticultural diseases and infestations (powdery mildew, downy mildew, and phylloxera) in the second half of the nineteenth century; second, by the tide of cheap bulk wine from the Midi and Algeria flooding shops and cafés in the 1920s. The fact that the language on the label of supposedly superior bottled wines often had little to do with the liquid inside further dulled the industry's luster. The first attempts to regulate wine quality had come before the First World War, when laws were passed specifying the areas within which certain wines could be produced. (These were accompanied by violent disputes concerning where the boundaries should be drawn, the most famous being the Champagne riots of 1911.) By the late 1920s, though, it had become clear that these were insufficient. Careless winemaking and the use of inferior grapes could render a wine's geographic origin largely irrelevant. What distinguished the INAO regulations, then, was their reach. In addition to defining appellation borders, the institute policed a host of viticultural and oenological practices—yield in the vineyard, for example, as well as pruning, sugar ripeness before harvest, time spent in the cellar before release, and so on. The rules applied only to a small percentage of wines. But these were the best wines, the ones that for centuries had made French wine famous, and would do so again.[6]

Étienne Nicolas sold those wines: classified growth Bordeaux, *cru* Burgundies, true Chablis and Champagne. *Mon Docteur le Vin* promoted them. "If you drink Chablis with your oysters," Derys writes, "you will never get typhoid fever." The message is plain: good wine, genuine wine, prevents illness. But the message also is nuanced. Dufy's accompanying illustration depicts a fashionably dressed family in a train station. They are taking a trip because the disease has broken out in their neighborhood, and the author faults them as "people who don't know that wine is the best preventative." Given Nicolas's clientele, can there be much doubt that Derys is speaking to readers as well? Dufy's sketches and watercolors depict an idealized haut-bourgeoisie world. Whether an afternoon at the horse races, a leisurely luncheon, or an excursion to an art gallery, they all seem to say to readers: "This is you," or rather "this could be you"—if only you were healthy and happy, if only you drank fine French wine.

That is the other part of the message. Not drinking French wine is detrimental to one's morals. Much of *Mon Docteur le Vin* seems lighthearted, and one can imagine Derys, Dufy, and Nicolas at work on it, all with tongues in proverbial cheeks. But there is nothing light about the handwritten "Homage au Vin" that introduces the volume. Penned by Marshal Philippe Pétain, it remembers the country's greatest glory as well as its greatest pain, the soldiers in the trenches twenty years earlier, fighting with their daily ration of wine, dying to defend the country of wine. To not drink wine, true French wine, is thus to damage the nation and defile their memory.

The passage of the initial INAO regulations did not immediately solve the crisis of French wine. War and occupation delayed its revival, as did the troubled economic times that followed. But by the 1950s, thanks in no small measure to all the rules that now guaranteed authenticity and eliminated fraud, France was once again the country to which all others looked when trying to make fine wine. And the controlled appellation system became the model that other nations emulated when trying to control viticulture. Not coincidentally, the Nicolas shops reinstituted the yearly luxury catalogues in 1949, with a new generation of artists, including Bernard Buffet, André Derain, and Kees van Dongen, commissioned to illustrate them. Meanwhile, overall wine consumption in France started to fall, as the government actively promoted quality rather than quantity. ("Drink better, drink less, drink longer," was an official slogan.[7]) Most important of all, the gap between cheap table wine and fine bottled wine, once gaping, began to narrow, with more and more *vin de pays* being made in the image of the best growths and *crus*. So too, in the 1960s and 1970s, when wine production exploded in New World countries such as Australia and the United States, vintners invariably looked to this new French model for inspiration. Bottled, premium wine rapidly became the worldwide rule, not a localized exception. Through all the changes, the Nicolas shops prospered. For as Étienne Nicolas had foreseen, people increasingly wanted to buy the sort of authentic wines he featured, the sort of wines that Gaston Derys and Raoul Dufy celebrated as being so good for body and soul. True wines, fine wines, French wines.

1. Alain Weill, *Nectar Comme Nicolas* (Paris: Editions Herscher, 1986), i.
2. Eugen Weber, *The Hollow Years: France in the 1930s* (New York: Norton, 1994), 71.
3. Ibid., 219.
4. Patricia Prestwich, *Drink and the Politics of Social Reform: Antialcoholism in France Since 1870* (Palo Alto, Calif.: Society for the Promotion of Science and Scholarship, 1988), 224–25.
5. Weber, *Hollow Years,* 70–73.
6. For a succinct review of this history, see: Hugh Johnson, *Vintage: The Story of Wine* (New York: Simon and Schuster, 1989), 436–43.
7. Prestwich, *Drink and the Politics of Social Reform,* 274.

Mon Docteur le Vin

(My Doctor, Wine)

1 *Wine as food*

At ten percent alcohol, a liter of wine contains 850 calories, or about a third of the daily requirement to maintain health and strength.

A liter of wine contains nutritional value equivalent to a pound of bread, six hundred grams of milk, a pound of meat, or a kilo of potatoes. Beer and cider contain a third of the calories of wine, while coffee with cream contains one-eighth.

Urban and rural people can and should drink a liter of unfortified wine per day with meals for their own good and the prosperity of the land.

DOCTOR LANDOUZY
dean, School of Medicine, Paris

Wine is the most hygienic and salutary beverage for workers in cities and the countryside. **DOCTOR POZZI**

When we drink wine, it first affects the digestive tract, then the nervous system, the major secretions, and finally nutrition. When it makes contact with the stomach, we experience a pleasant warmth, then a feeling of regained strength.

PROFESSOR ARNOZAN
School of Medicine, University of Bordeaux

— WHAT? ALREADY AWAKE? AND THERE I WAS THINKING THAT PERFORMERS ALWAYS SLEEP LATE.

— FILM IS A DICTATOR THAT HAS RUINED EVERYTHING. I'M AT THE STUDIO AT 8 IN THE MORNING AND ACT UNTIL AFTER NOON. THEN AFTER LUNCH, I ACT SOME MORE. IN THE EVENING, I ACT ONSTAGE.

— HOW DO YOU MANAGE?

— I EAT AND DRINK CORRECTLY. AT THE STUDIO WHERE I OFTEN HAVE LUNCH, I EVEN HAVE BORDEAUX WINE DELIVERED, WHICH AGREES WITH ME AND HAPPILY MAKES UP FOR THE CALORIES I'M BURNING.

— I CAN'T TAKE IT, YOU NEVER WANT TO GO OUT WITH ME ANY MORE. WHAT'S THE USE OF BEING MARRIED?

— POOR DEAR, YOU KNOW HOW TIRED I AM, I JUST DON'T FEEL LIKE DOING ANYTHING.

— IT'S YOUR MISERABLE DIET OF COOKED GRASS, WATER, AND NEVER A DROP OF WINE. JUST TO KEEP YOUR EMACIATED FIGURE. MIGHT BE BETTER TO TRY TO KEEP YOUR HUSBAND.

Vitamins
and the radioactivity
of wine

A lack of vitamins exposes the body to grave ailments like scurvy, rickets, and beriberi. Doctor Portier's scholarly research has shown that wine contains vitamins, particularly antiscorbutic vitamin Cs and nourishing vitamin Bs.

These vitamins harmonize the endocrinal functions and those of the vegetative nervous system. They stimulate secretion of digestive juices, and enhance the intestine's tone and motor function, as well as regulating muscle tone in general, the function of the skin in nourishment, and immune reactions.

PROFESSOR LORENZINI
University of Milan

Moreover, wine is a remarkable radioactive foodstuff, for grapes store solar radiation and devour mineral elements from the soil.

Exactly because of its radioactive properties, wine stimulates the vital functions, organs and glands, increases the vitality of the tissues, augments the red blood cell count, positively influences the nutritional process, and regulates the tone of the vagosympathetic system.

DOCTOR F. DOUGNAC

3 Wine

and

childhood ailments

Doctor Lorenzini of the University of Milan has shown that the vitamins in wine are necessary for growth.

A small quantity of wine acts on children as it does on adults, aiding gastric secretions during the ingestion of food. Wine is a stimulant for the mind and reflexes, a means to healthful warmth, and therefore must encourage the digestive process. During childhood, when the body needs materials to aid in building tissue, wine's ingredients contribute vitally important elements, both organic and mineral, to this process.

PROFESSOR L. DIEULAFÉ
School of Medicine, University of Toulouse

Dieulafé adds that for children, wine provides an easily assimilated form of phosphorus that is not found in even the best pharmaceutical preparations.

— HEAVENS, YOUR KIDS ARE LITTLE DEVILS, AREN'T THEY, SISTER?

— THAT'S BETTER THAN BEING SICKLY. YOU CAN BET WE GIVE THEM A DROP OF WINE. MY BOSS SAYS IT HELPS THEIR BONES DEVELOP AND BRINGS SUNSHINE TO THEIR HEARTS.

— HE'S RIGHT: AT SCHOOL THEY TAUGHT US THAT KING HENRI IV WAS DRINKING JURANÇON WINE FROM THE CRADLE ON. MAYBE THAT'S HOW HE BECAME SUCH A LUSTY OLD CODGER.

— HEY, ARE YOU OFF ON HOLIDAY?

— OLD FRIEND, THERE'S AN OUTBREAK OF TYPHOID FEVER IN THE NEIGHBORHOOD.
  MORE PEOPLE WHO DON'T KNOW THAT WINE IS THE BEST PREVENTATIVE AGAINST TYPHOID FEVER!

Wine as a treatment
for *typhoid fever*

It has been scientifically proven that wine kills the bacterium that causes typhoid fever in a matter of minutes. If you drink Chablis with your oysters, you will never get typhoid fever. All doctors agree on this since Dr. Pick of the Health Institute of Vienna proved that the microbe for typhoid fever is killed by unwatered wine in a few minutes, while the microbe for cholera is killed in five minutes. He concluded that a cup of water full of cholera bacteria might be drunk without harm after being cut with a third of a cup of wine for the period of five minutes.

After meticulous and convincing observations, Petit and Pinard observed wine's remarkable nutritive value against typhoid fever in its adynamic state.

RAYMOND BRUNET

Behier prescribed heavy doses of aromatic wines, not only for cases of typhoid fever, but for a number of serious illnesses.

DOCTOR F. DOUGNAC

Wine is an excellent prophylactic and even curative measure for infectious diseases, eruptive diseases, intermittent fevers, and typhoid fever.

DOCTOR PETON

5 *Wine for healthy kidneys*

The beneficial effect of wine on the kidneys and even the liver is undeniable.

Moreover, since Old Testament times, these therapeutic values of wine have been known.

Hippocrates recommended wine for patients with dropsy, and white wine was considered more diuretic than red.

White wine in particular, which contains a considerable amount of tartrates, is a powerful diuretic.
DOCTOR ÉDOUARD BAZEROLLE

In 1935 Doctor H. Gahlinger, a consultant at Châtel-Guyon, published a noteworthy study, *Wine and Urinary Colibacillosis*. He believes that if this ailment occurs more often in women patients, it's because they generally drink less wine. He cites a case that is both inarguable and amusing. A woman suffering from that dangerous ailment was to have one of her kidneys removed. To amuse the woman before her major surgery, her friends invited her to a series of gourmet dinners, which of course included good wines. As a result, the patient was cured and surgery avoided.

— HEY, STAND UP STRAIGHT! THOSE YOUNG LADIES ARE LOOKING AT YOU. EVEN IF YOU ARE THIRTY AND A GONCOURT PRIZE–WINNING NOVELIST, FOR SOME WOMEN WHAT COUNTS IS YOUR PHYSIQUE.

— THE GONCOURT PRIZE DOESN'T KEEP MY KIDNEYS FROM HURTING ME.

— YOU AND YOUR HURT KIDNEYS! HERE'S SOME ADVICE: TRY A DIET OF THE LOCAL WINE. IN ALSACE, WHERE PEOPLE TAKE CARE TO CLEANSE THEIR SYSTEMS WITH WHITE WINE, NO ONE HAS KIDNEY PROBLEMS.

— MOM WANTED ME TO MARRY THAT GUY! NOT ON YOUR LIFE! HE WAS BORN TIRED. WHAT'S IN IT FOR ME?

— HE WAS ALSO BORN A MILLIONAIRE. HIS FATHER OWNS THE IRONWORKS OF LA GRANDE JATTE.

— WHO CARES? THAT BOY IS WHISTLING IN THE DARK. YESTERDAY I POURED HIM A SPLENDID ROMANÉE, AND HE LEFT HIS GLASS UNTOUCHED. THAT WOULD ALREADY BE A CRIME FOR SOMEONE IN GOOD HEALTH. FOR AN ANEMIC CASE LIKE HIM, IT'S A DOUBLE CRIME! I WANT A REAL HUSBAND!

Wine
as a treatment for
depression and anemia

Wine is a heroic remedy for what Bouchardat called physiological worries, namely depression or withering away.

DOCTOR F. DOUGNAC

Dougnac cites the case of an American teetotaler who was cured of his fatigue and neurasthenia by Saint-Émilion. He also notes that wine contains iron, phosphorus, and many other elements we are not aware of, in the lively and easily assimilated form of enzymes, vitamins, and radioactive substances.

When it's taken in reasonable measure, wine always positively affects the morale as well as muscular activity and strength.

DOCTOR J. ALQUIER

Wine is indicated above all in nervous afflictions lacking any organic bases, especially those arising from poor morale, such as longings and hypochondria.

DOCTOR FONSSAGRIVES

Anemics and convalescents cannot do without wine.

DOCTOR PETON

7 *Wine*

as a treatment

for appendicitis

Wine is a great enemy of microbes. It attacks those in the intestines and elsewhere.

Appendicitis has become considerably more common since the phylloxera crisis, which resulted in the adulteration of wine and increased the habit of water drinking.

DOCTOR GAGEY

Doctor Gagey studied the case of a family of sixteen, including five siblings with children who lived separately. During a period of four years, six of them underwent surgery for appendicitis. These six people were precisely those in the family who drank only water.

Drinker of water, subject to appendicitis.

DOCTOR BOUCHARD

— WHAT'S BECOME OF MADAME DE Z.? WE NEVER SEE HER ANY MORE.

— SHE'S IN THE HOSPITAL WITH A FINE CASE OF APPENDICITIS.

— AND SHE NEVER DRINKS ANYTHING BUT WATER!

— MY HUSBAND SAYS THAT'S THE REASON!

— LISTEN, YOUR FRIEND IS DRINKING AND PUTTING AWAY PLENTY OF FOOD, CONSIDERING HE'S A DIABETIC.

— HIS DOCTOR NOT ONLY PERMITS HIM TO DRINK BORDEAUX BUT EVEN PRESCRIBES IT.

Wine

as a treatment

for diabetes

A good wine, rather mellow, from the Bordeaux, Burgundy, or Tours region is an unbeatable tonic.

DOCTOR PETON

Today, no one argues with Bouchardat's opinion that a moderate amount of wine is healthful for diabetics.

LOEPER AND ALQUIER

Because of its alcohol content, wine works as a nourishing food and partially replaces necessary carbohydrates without adding sugar or exceeding the usage factor of these substances. That was the opinion of During of Hamburg, whose treatment for diabetes by prescribing red wine in moderate doses was very popular in Germany.

DOCTOR F. DOUGNAC

For this treatment, Professor Marcel Labbé voiced a preference for Bordeaux wines.

9 *Wine*
as a remedy for convalescents

A fine old wine can work real miracles in cases of severe illness, even a wasting disease.

More than iron, cinchona, arsenic, kola, and phosophates, wine can build up a disturbed diet and revive fading strength.

As a patient ingests the precious nectar, he feels correctly that his strength is returning: the slowly recovering typhoid patient; the malaria victim who has managed to survive infection; the diphtheria case who has just been saved; the invalid weakened by scarlet fever or smallpox.

PROFESSOR ARNOZAN
School of Medicine, Bordeaux

For convalescents recovering from lengthy illnesses, wine is as useful as clear soup; both compensate for deficiencies of the organism.

DOCTOR BOUCHARDAT

In his thesis, Doctor Dougnac proves that many patients, convalescents, and sufferers from exhaustion who stuff themselves with pills, powders, and tablets would find an old Bordeaux to be a faster remedy to recuperate their strength.

PROFESSOR G. PORTMANN
School of Medicine, Bordeaux

— WHAT DO WE GIVE TO GRAVELY ILL PATIENTS AND SURGICAL CASES IN HOSPITALS? VOLTAIRE SAW CHAMPAGNE
AS OUR COUNTRY'S FORM OF LAUGHTER:
"OF OUR FRENCH FOLK THE IMAGE BEAMING
IN THIS COLD WINE WITH BUBBLES GLEAMING . . . "

— THE BRIDE IS DELIGHTFUL—WHAT A SMILE!

— AND HAPPY AS A LARK. WHICH IS UNDERSTANDABLE. HER FATHER IS FROM BEAUNE AND HER MOTHER FROM SAINT-
  ÉMILION, SO THEY HAVE ONE OF THE FINEST WINE CELLARS IN FRANCE. THAT YOUNGSTER IS A DAUGHTER OF THE
  VINE.

How wine affects the disposition

The moderate use of good quality wine is certainly not forbidden for bodily health and may even be recommended for the disposition.

PROFESSOR LÉON BERNARD
member of the Academy of Medicine
professor, School of Medicine, Paris

Wine makes our mood joyous, sharpens our judgment, and makes us inclined to be affectionate by delighting the senses, warming the heart, and stimulating the brain.

PROFESSOR POUSSON
School of Medicine, Bordeaux

It's the essence of joy and health, the extract of Gallic humor, a reflection of that gentle country France.

RAYMOND POINCARÉ

11 *How*

wine affects

the morale

During the First World War, wine allowed the fighting men to endure the ordeals of the trenches. That's what kept their morale and hopes alive.

PROFESSOR POUSSON
School of Medicine, Bordeaux

The sustained consumption of wine has certainly contributed to the formation and development of some fundamental qualities of the breed: cordiality, frankness, and gaiety, which differ profoundly from those peoples who are beer drinkers.

HENRI BABINSKI

Wine inspires gaiety, strength, youth, and health. It is bottled sunshine.
PROFESSOR P. PIERRET

— SO YOU'RE NOT GETTING DIVORCED?

— I FOLLOWED THE ADVICE OF AN OLD COUNTRY COUSIN WHO TOLD ME, "IF YOUR HUSBAND IS BORED WITH YOU,
   IT'S BECAUSE YOU EAT AND DRINK SO BADLY AT HOME." SINCE I STARTED SERVING HIM GOOD WINE, PIERRE IS
   HAPPY, FULL OF GUSTO, AND ENJOYS HIMSELF AT HOME.

— HE CAPTURED THAT ODD, FIXED STARE QUITE WELL.

— YOU KNOW, SHE TAKES DRUGS.

— WHAT DO YOU MEAN? AT DINNER SHE ONLY DRINKS WATER!

— PRECISELY!

Downfall
of a lady teetotaler

At the Academy of Medicine, Professor Guillain denounced society alcoholism—the sneaky intoxication with cocktails and other poisons that grabs hold of certain well-bred, snobbish women who are habitual water drinkers.

Deprived of wine, Americans have sought a replacement in opium. A League of Nations study has proven that the United States is the world's largest consumer of opium.

PROFESSOR CAMBIAIRE
Lincoln Memorial University

Who is unaware of the ravages of alcoholism? They are frightful! The horrible plague attacks the body, mind, moral being, and family. Wine drinkers do not drink spirits. In wine country, there are very few alcoholics.

PROFESSOR A. GAUTIER
Academy of Medicine and Sciences

In the sixth century A.D., there was complete prohibition in China. In a few years the country, which had been an immense wine producer, became a vast field of poppies. The Chinese poisoned themselves with opium, since they could no longer drink wine.

DOCTOR F. DOUGNAC

13 *Wine as a treatment for obesity*

Water tends to thicken the flesh. Indeed, fat is formed and intervenes in water drinkers, to neutralize the poisons deriving from food that are not destroyed by internal secretions. These secretions are insufficient due to the lack of a stimulant like wine.

Matters are quite different for moderate drinkers of wine, which acts beneficially on the glands that burn food residue. Moreover, Doctor Dougnac has shown that these glands, which secrete hormones that destroy waste, perform far better when stimulated by wine:

They defend themselves more energetically against the autointoxication caused by migraine, eczema, gout, and obesity.

Professor Armand Gautier of the Academy of Medicine agrees that wine augments the body's defenses, allowing a stronger resistance to autointoxication, depression, and obesity.

Moderate wine drinkers are thin because they burn off their waste products.

DOCTOR CHARLES FIESSINGER

— BUT MY DEAR, YOU'VE LEFT A FULL GLASS OF THIS VINTAGE WINE—IT'S CRIMINAL!

— I'VE HAD A TASTE AND DID IT JUSTICE, BUT THEY SAY WINE IS FATTENING AND I'M WATCHING MY WEIGHT.

— WHAT A DISMAL ERROR! MODERN SCIENCE DOES NOT AGREE WITH YOU. I SUGGEST YOU READ DOCTOR FRANÇOIS DOUGNAC'S STUDY ON WINE.

— WHO WOULD SUSPECT THAT THEY ARE MOTHER AND DAUGHTER?

— NO KIDDING! YOU COULD SWEAR THEY WERE SISTERS.

— THEY'RE WOMEN FROM THE CHAMPAGNE REGION, OLD BOY, WHO KEEP YOUNG AND FIT WITH THE JUICE OF THE
   GRAPE.

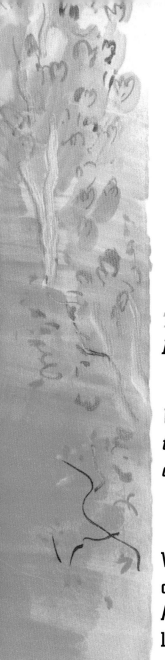

Wine
maintains youth
and beauty

The most beautiful and charming women are found in France, Spain, and Italy, all wine countries.

DOCTOR F. DOUGNAC

Wine revives strength and acts as a heroic remedy, better than any medical tonic like iron, cinchona, arsenic, kola, or nux vomica.

PROFESSOR G. PORTMANN
School of Medicine, Bordeaux

Wine takes its revenge on those who don't drink it by covering their faces with acne, pimples, and red blotches. Aristophanes was so right when he exclaimed, "Wine is like milk for Aphrodite."

From the moment women take to wine, water receives a death sentence. Soon, there's no need to open the handbag to get lipstick. Lips and cheeks naturally acquire an enticing glow.

HENRY BORDEAUX
Académie française

15 *Wine is essential for writers*

One of the best ways to compare the intellectual powers of citizens of different countries is to study the list of Nobel Prize winners.

PROFESSOR CAMBIAIRE

By citing statistics, Professor Cambiaire proves that most Nobel laureates are scholars or writers from wine-drinking countries.

If wine vanished from human production, I believe that a void would open up in health and intellect, a defection, a vacuum much more frightful than all the abuses and deviations that wine is accused of causing.

CHARLES BAUDELAIRE

Wine taken in moderation is a muscle tonic and mental stimulant.

DOCTOR WIDAL
Member of the Institute

— THE POOR FELLOW IS DONE FOR.

— THE PLAY HE WROTE IS IDIOTIC. WHAT A SLAP IN THE FACE!

— I HAD DINNER WITH HIM THE OTHER DAY AND HE WAS DRINKING WATER. THAT'S INTELLECTUAL SUICIDE!

— THAT RUBENS IS MAGNIFICENT. FOR SURE, THE FLEMISH . . .

— THEY CERTAINLY ARE BRILLIANT, BUT WITHOUT OUR BURGUNDY, THEY WOULD HAVE GOTTEN NOWHERE.

Wine
is necessary
for artists

Countries where authentic art is produced are wine countries, and as for Flanders, no imbibers ever possessed better cellars of Burgundy wine than those in this region.

The stimulating effect of wine on mental activity is too well known for me to speak of it again here. Most brilliant authors, musicians, poets, and artists were and are wine lovers and imbibers. Need I mention that Gluck used to compose under the influence of a bottle of champagne? Or that Beethoven adored white wines from the Rhine region and near Vienna?

DOCTOR PAUL RAMAIN

Since ancient times, the arts, letters, and sciences have flourished in all lands whose people consume a moderate amount of wine.

CHARLES DORMONTAL

As Professor Barrius correctly noticed and pointed out emphatically, the only place where civilization flowers spontaneously is vineyard country.

17 *Wine is essential for athletes*

If animals, especially horses, are given wine to drink, they are easily motivated to work harder, as shown by laboratory experiments and in daily life, proving that wine is an admirable stimulant. Professor Armand Gautier cites the case of a mule that stubbornly refused to move when given a load too heavy for its liking. Just when the animal was about to be disposed of, a servant suggested giving it two liters of wine per day. This advice was followed, and thereafter the mule did excellent work.

Experiments carried out in the armies of Europe show that moderate doses of wine not only allow soldiers to easily accomplish the often excessive work required of them, but even protect them from sickness and disease that often strikes those deprived of it.

PROFESSOR ARMAND GAUTIER
Academy of Medicine and Academy of Sciences

Since Prohibition, the Americans have retrogressed in sports. They have lost their superiority in world boxing championships, and could only maintain their superiority in foot races over short distances.

PROFESSOR CAMBIAIRE

— IT'S ALL OVER! TOM BIER WILL MAKE SHORT WORK OF HIM.

— I BET ANYTHING YOU LIKE THAT THE FRENCHMAN WILL KNOCK OUT YOUR TOM BIER.

— WHAT DO YOU MEAN?

— BECAUSE HE HAS AN AMAZING WINE CELLAR! AND GOOD WINE BUILDS UP MUSCLE.

— I'VE NEVER SEEN SUCH FINE-LOOKING MEN!

— THAT'S HOW IT IS EVERYWHERE IN THE BURGUNDY REGION.

Wine

makes

a fine figure

of a man

According to the statistics categorized for 1931 and 1932 by Doctor François Dougnac, for the same number of births, 36,617 young men in wine-growing regions were found fit for military service, whereas only 29,467 qualified in other regions.

In France, at the medical board for recruiting, we were able to note that among the young men called for army duty, those from wine-growing regions were the most muscular, alert, and lithe, as well as strongest, biggest, and leanest.

DOCTOR AMERLINCK

Vineyards provide more soldiers to the homeland than any other form of farming.

DOCTOR J. GUYOT

Doctor Dougnac's statistics

OUT OF 1,000 INHABITANTS	OVER SIXTY	OVER SEVENTY
In wine-drinking regions	216	87
In beer-drinking regions	165	68
In cider-drinking regions	134	51

Statistics from Monsieur Cordier, mayor of Saint-Julien

INHABITANTS PER 100,000 POPULATION, BY AGE:

IN ALL OF FRANCE		IN THE MÉDOC REGION
4,661	60–64 years	6,259
3,644	65–69	5,000
4,359	70–79	6,550
1,053	80 and older	1,981

Finally, let's mention the magnificent example of Doctor Guéniot. At the age of 102, the venerable senior member of the Academy of Medicine wrote to Doctor Dougnac that he benefited greatly from drinking wine with his meals every day. In his admirable book, *Living to Be One Hundred,* Doctor Guéniot paid tribute to the virtues of wine.

Luncheon in Paris with Raoul Dufy

Henry McBride

My meeting with Raoul Dufy in Paris a year after the war had begun had an amusing touch of surprise.

I had asked young Lieut. Malye, one of James Stephens' friends, to dinner, and when I came home at 7 the domestique said a soldier had just been calling for me who had said that he would return for me in a few minutes. Thinking of course that it had been Malye, I sauntered out on the avenue to seek him. Just in front of the house under the trees an officer had propped a rebellious motorcyclette upon a rack and it was racing away like mad although standing still. The explosions were terrific. M. Malye not being visible, I joined the little crowd around the exploding bicycle.

Suddenly a young soldier who had been assisting the Lieutenant of the bicycle stepped forward and said, "Is this Mr. McBride?" and when I had replied "yes," explained that he was Raoul Dufy. He had just learned that I was in Paris and had come at once to thank me for the kind things I had written about him in *The Sun* the year before.

The people in my house and the neighboring houses, brought to the window by the noise, appeared to be vastly astonished at my share in this military maneuver, which was increased by the arrival of my dinner guest, whom the simple soldiers in the throng, including Dufy, had to salute. The troublesome motorcyclette finally became adjusted and bore its Lieutenant away. Dufy could not dine with me, as his wife would be alarmed at his absence on the day of his "perme" (all soldiers, young and old, having immediately shortened the word "permission" to "perme") so I agreed to lunch with him and Mme. Dufy on July 14. Dufy's depot is not far from Paris. He is in a bicycle corps, he explained, and that was how he happened to assist the military cyclist in distress in front of my house. He had an afternoon off once in two weeks.

His studio is in Montmartre, in the neighborhood of the Place Pigalle, and it is full of works that America has not yet seen, but would profit by seeing; but before looking at them we ate an excellent luncheon. The plat was a work of art in itself, a roast surrounded by four vegetables of harmonious colors. The dish was decidedly worthy of being painted by M. Dufy. It struck me afterward as strange that M. Dufy, who is fond of still lifes, had never painted such a plat. Being devoted to food myself, I imagined that in the presence of such a piece de resistance the primitive artiste's emotions—M. Dufy is a primitive—are so aroused that there is no withstanding the imperative desire to "kill the thing one loves" and so every perfect steak surrounded by vegetables gets immediately eaten instead of painted. Certainly none of the modern primitives paints them. They all paint lemons and bananas.

There is a bottle of red wine on the table, but as we were about to sit down M. Dufy said: "Perhaps Monsieur McBride would like white wine; we have some specially good white wine," and without waiting to hear from me he immediately arose and returned with a bottle of cobwebby white. Now I have always noticed that when every work of an artist contains something that is personally pleasant I am sure to find the artist himself simpatico. Once again it proved true. How did he know I like white wine and always drank it in preference? Simply by intuition lui et moi being simpatico.

In the atelier were stacks of canvases, some of them very large. All that I like best had been painted in the Midi, gardens and balconies in the cavalier method of the moderns, but recognizable as gardens and balconies just the same. Dufy's color is always good, design good, and it can be felt that he could be realistic if he wished. He is not a primitif because he doesn't know how to paint, but for quite the contrary reason, because he does know how to paint.

He asked me how I stood on the question of Picasso and Matisse and was not horrified at my reply that I never found their work completely successful, though always completely interesting. (We were talking of the abstract performances by these men. Afterward I found abstractions by them that to me were completely successful.) M. Dufy said there were no new names to place beside theirs. For him Matisse has awakened a new interest in painting, which was a great thing. Apparently everything had been said, but Matisse found new ways to say it. Picasso was trying for problems that were perhaps insolvable, but his experiments had that interest.

He showed me a box of silks and damasks printed from his designs, most of them from the "Bestiare," the book of wood prints with text by Apollinaire. Apollinaire, full of fantasy and an amusing fellow, both M. and Mme. Dufy agreed. Dufy had designed stuffs for Poiret. Both Poiret and he felt that the war would not sidetrack modern art. Never could go back to the old, at least. For his part, if he did war things they would be allegorical. Give me a silk pochette of his design, with all the Allies mounted upon white horses. He said Braque had become a soldier, had found himself in the vie militaire. M. and Mme. Dufy said that last year in the first week in September there was an anxious moment. "Heard the cannon, you know," most impressively. "We heard the cannon of the Germans, and in the papers, next day, not a word! We looked to see what had happened—nothing!" Dufy comes from Normandy. His ancestors being originally Irish, hence the name. There had also been a German intermarriage among his progenitors, nevertheless, with a smile and a military salute: "J'èspere que je suis un bon français!"

New York, *The Sun,* December 30, 1917

Acknowledgments

Max Miltzlaff was Henry McBride's close friend for many years and took care of McBride until his death in 1961. I was fortunate to meet Max when I purchased a home from him in 1987, and we became close friends in the years following. As part of the purchase I inherited "stuff" that Max could not fit into his retirement home in Florida. Being the pack rat that I am, I took everything he offered and stored it in the basement. Needless to say, the day came when the cache outgrew the basement and some "stuff" had to go. So in the year 2000 I systematically started to sort and pack.

I had previously returned to Max some treasures I had found among his belongings, so I was careful to check out items before discarding them. One strange find was a framed page from a book. Had sentimentalism inspired Max to frame a page? Just in case a treasure lurked behind the page, and before it became fodder for the charity shop, I broke open the frame. Treasure was indeed there—a whole book was in the frame—a perfectly preserved book, with stunning illustrations. The book was *Mon Docteur le Vin.*

Max did not remember why or when he had framed the book, but when the decision was made to reproduce the book in English, Max did the first translation. While working on the translation he became convinced that a glass of wine was beneficial to one's well-being, and he took "wine with meals" literally. He swears that it has cured a few ills, and who are we to disagree with a man looking ahead to his one hundredth birthday in 2003?

I would like to thank Max Miltzlaff for introducing me to the wonderful writings of Henry McBride, and I thank Henry McBride himself, whom I never knew in life but whose life has influenced mine. Thanks to the truly exceptional talent of Raoul Dufy and to his estate for being so gracious in allowing the Foundation to reproduce *Mon Docteur le Vin,* and to Michael Spizzirri for pulling this all together, Christine Lawrence-Bell for her attention to detail, and Karina Dimidjian and Ed Schaffzin for giving me faith in attorneys. Last, but certainly not least, a team of people who deserve much more than praise . . . wine maybe? . . . at Yale University Press: Jonathan Brent, who believed in the book as much as we did and without whom this would not have become a reality; Candice Nowlin (you can work for me anytime); Linda Klein; Julianne Griffin; and Dan Heaton . . . thank you all for helping to bring the wit and verve of the original into print again.

Oh, and by the way, the illustration in the frame—that is what you now see on the jacket of this book!

CHRISTIEN A. DUCKER

Trustee

The Henry McBride Foundation

HENRY McBRIDE (1867–1962), the American art critic, is a figure so unlike any of his successors in the last decades of the twentieth century that it now requires a certain leap of historical imagination to think our way back to his exemplary career in the first half of that century. Almost everything we now take for granted on the contemporary art scene did not yet exist when McBride embarked on his critical endeavors. . . . The abundant, well-appointed dealers' galleries that now regularly bring us a vast range of new talent; the many well-established museums that boast of first-rate collections of the modernist classics while at the same time competing for the privilege of being the first to embrace new artistic developments; the friendly reception that is now accorded to even the most far-out innovations in art by critics in the mainstream press . . . all of this came much later, and in part as a result of the pioneering efforts of a very small circle of artists and intellectuals. In that circle, McBride was the premier critic of the modernist movement. What so many others at the time found shocking and even repulsive in modernist art, McBride had the wit—and the aesthetic intelligence—to see as the classics of the future, and he had the good fortune to live long enough to see his judgment vindicated. To remain unacquainted with that voice today is to miss out on some of the most intelligent criticism that the era of early modernism has bequeathed to us—and to miss out on some of the intellectual fun of that era as well.

Hilton Kramer, *The Flow of Art*
The Henry McBride Series in Modernism and Modernity

RAOUL DUFY (1877–1953), who was born in Le Havre, said, "My youth was cradled by music and the sea." His father was an accomplished musician whose passion for music was ultimately recalled by Dufy in lively pen-and-ink studies. Dufy was trained at the École des Beaux-Arts in Paris, where early in his career he associated with the artists who became known as the Fauves, and in 1908 he briefly fell under the influence of early Cubism. He is perhaps best known as a society painter, the witty recorder of the fashionable world of his time— vivacious and entertaining scenes, often of boating or parties. But Dufy's paintings were just one element of his extraordinary artistic versatility. In watercolors, ceramics, engravings, tapestries and fabrics, stage sets and furniture, his ability to deftly trace brilliantly conceived lines and colors makes him one of the great French Moderns. In 1930 he won the Pittsburgh Carnegie Prize; in 1936 large exhibitions of his work were shown in New York and London; and in 1950, three years before his death, while visiting New York and Boston for medical treatment for arthritis, he painted the Brooklyn Bridge, Times Square, and Fenway Park—thereby securing America's place in his timeless collection of art.

GASTON DERYS is a pseudonym for Gaston Colomb, who, under many aliases, was a prolific writer and well-known French gastronome. His other books include *Oú déjeunerons-nous à Paris?* (1937), *L'Art d'être gourmand* (1929), and *Les grandes amoreuses.* He cowrote *Anthologie de la gastronomie française* and *Gaiétes et Curiosités gastronomiques* with fellow French gastronome and writer Maurice Edmond Saillant (known as Curnonsky).